Laughter and smiles as the Queen and the Duke of Edinburgh leave a service of thanksgiving at St George's Chapel at Windsor Castle to mark the 660th anniversary of the founding of the Order of the Garter and the College of St George and the 60th anniversary of the reintroduction of the annual Garter service by King George VI. This picture was taken on April 23, 2008, two days after the Queen's 82nd birthday.

Introduction

Their wedding was the culmination of a fairy-tale romance between a beautiful princess and a tall, charming naval officer.

After the Second World War, as Britain recovered and forged a new peacetime future, the country's collective pulse was quickened by the announcement that Princess Elizabeth and Prince Philip were to marry.

Together they passed many milestones – her coronation, the arrival of their four children, her Silver, Golden and Diamond Jubilee celebrations; the birth of grandchildren and great-grandchildren; travel to numerous Commonwealth countries and significant events up and down the British Isles; their own diamond wedding.

The royal partnership has endured more than 70 years, surviving many of the trials and tribulations that can befall families across the country, but which are not played out so glaringly in the public eye.

This special publication pays tribute to Prince Philip, Duke of Edinburgh, whose unerring support for the Queen – from her accession to the throne in 1953 to her Diamond Jubilee and subsequent 90th birthday celebrations – has earned him a prominent place in the history books.

It features numerous long-forgotten photographs of people who found a great deal of pleasure in meeting the Duke, from the working man and the busy mum to the leaders of some of the world's most powerful nations. Actors, musicians, comedians and entertainers lit up the pages of daily newspapers as the Duke toured the country, meeting and greeting a host of celebrities during his engagements, often related to his work with the Duke of Edinburgh Awards.

We hope you enjoy delving into this publication, which brings back many memories of the fashions, the people, the hopes and the happenings of a royal life spanning many decades.

EDITOR A̶ ̶
Pauline H̶̶

PRODUCT̶̶
Dan Sharp̶

DESIGNER̶
Craig Lam̶
design_lamb@btinternet.com

COVER DESIGN:
Holly Furness

REPROGRAPHICS:
Paul Fincham and
Jonathan Schofield

PUBLISHER:
Steve O'Hara

PUBLISHING DIRECTOR:
Dan Savage

COMMERCIAL DIRECTOR:
Nigel Hole

MARKETING MANAGER:
Charlotte Park
cpark@mortons.co.uk

DISTRIBUTION:
tradesales@mortons.co.uk
classicmagazines.co.uk/tradesales

PRINTED BY:
William Gibbons and Sons,
Wolverhampton

ISBN:
978-1-911276-23-4

PUBLISHED BY:
Mortons Media Group Ltd,
Media Centre, Morton Way,
Horncastle, Lincolnshire
LN9 6JR.
Tel: 01507 529529

COPYRIGHT:
Mortons Media Group Ltd, 2017
All rights reserved.

Cambridge connection: the Duke was in Cambridge on February 12, 2009, where he unveiled a plaque naming a train *University of Cambridge* to mark the 800th anniversary of the world-famous seat of learning.

Contents

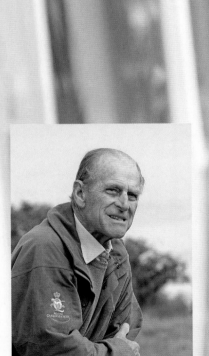

INSET: The Duke of Edinburgh during a tour of battlefields in the Crimea, Ukraine, on October 23, 2004. As Colonel in Chief of the Queen's Royal Hussars, the Duke was commemorating the 150th anniversary of the Charge of the Light Brigade. The 83-year-old royal joined a coach party of regimental top brass touring the battlefields of the Crimean War with Russia, visiting the battlefield at Balaclava where, in 1854, courageous British cavalrymen rode to their deaths in the infamous Light Brigade charge.

IMAGE CREDITS:
PRESS ASSOCIATION IMAGES, PAIMAGES.CO.UK
Unless otherwise stated, the images in this publication are courtesy of the Press Association.

First born: Princess Elizabeth and the Duke of Edinburgh hold their first child Prince Charles, aged six months. The photograph was taken on April 26, 1949.

Who remembers the long, hot summer of 1976? The Queen and the Duke of Edinburgh, pictured during their traditional summer break at Balmoral Castle, in September of that year.

The Queen presents a delighted Duke with New Zealand's highest honour, the Order of New Zealand, at Buckingham Palace on June 6, 2013.

Look of love: the couple gaze contentedly into each other's eyes as they celebrate their diamond wedding anniversary in November 2007 at Broadlands, where they spent their wedding night 60 years previously.

November 20, 1947: the couple wave to the crowds from the balcony of Buckingham Palace after their wedding.

An extraordinary life

Dashing, tall and handsome, he captured the heart of a princess who would one day become Queen. Prince Philip, the Duke of Edinburgh, has stood proudly and loyally by his wife's side since their wedding on a November day in 1947. Despite the turmoil of the Second World War, the couple's teenage friendship blossomed into romance and Princess Elizabeth's joy was complete when she walked down the aisle of Westminster Abbey to join her husband-to-be at the altar.

There followed the unexpectedly early and sudden loss of her father, King George VI, in 1952 – but from Elizabeth's subsequent coronation emerged a triumphant reign which saw the royal couple travel all over the globe, meeting kings and queens, prime ministers and presidents, witnessing the terms in office of numerous heads of state begin and come to an end.

Over those seven decades the Duke of Edinburgh has been at the Queen's side through times good and bad – happiness at the birth of their four children; sadness when the marriages of Charles to Diana, Anne to Captain Mark Phillips and Andrew to Sarah Ferguson ended in divorce.

He was there to comfort the Queen during her 'annus horribilis', which saw Windsor Castle engulfed by fire in November 1992, just days after their 45th wedding anniversary, and supported her at crucial times, including following the death of Diana, Princess of Wales, in August 1997.

Sometimes controversial, occasionally brusque, often entertaining and always smartly dressed, the Duke of Edinburgh played a prominent role in the British monarchy during the 20th and 21st centuries, providing it with a backbone of staunch dependability.

That role as the head of 'The Firm', as he reputedly dubbed the royal family, gave the Queen someone to confide in and provided a metaphorical, and maybe physical at times, shoulder to cry on.

The part he has played in the dynasty cannot be underestimated and within the pages of this special publication we look back with admiration and warmth at the achievements, the celebrations, the successes and the occasional faux pas that made the Duke of Edinburgh an integral and unforgettable part of the House of Windsor.

Taken by royal command on April 26, 1949, this happy picture shows the Duke of Edinburgh with his infant son, Prince Charles, in a private room at Buckingham Palace.

A magical family moment, as Prince Charles and Princess Anne are pushed on a swing by their father, the Duke of Edinburgh, with their mother looking on, in the grounds of Balmoral on September 14, 1955.

May 4, 1953: The Duke of Edinburgh in the cockpit of an aircraft at White Waltham airfield in Berkshire, when he made his last three flights before qualifying for his Royal Air Force wings.

Unnoticed by passers-by, the Duke of Edinburgh, Renter Warden of the Fishmongers' Hall, crosses the pavement near Billingsgate Market, after he had paid a surprise visit to the market, London's great fish distribution centre, on March 31, 1960. He had spent an hour and a quarter watching the market at work, having arrived there at 7.30am.

December 1, 1982: The Duke of Edinburgh, as senior colonel of the Household Division, pins the South Atlantic Medal on Guardsman Simon Weston, from Gwent, at Buckingham Palace in London. Guardsman Weston was wounded during the attack on the *Sir Galahad* during the Falklands War.

The Duke of Edinburgh steps from the driving seat of an experimental 120mph glass-roofed Reliant Scimitar estate car at London Airport on May 2, 1966, en route to Oslo for a two-day visit to the British Trade Fair and Fortnight.

The Duke of Edinburgh takes the tiller of his yacht *Bluebottle* at Cowes, Isle of Wight, on August 3, 1960, before competing in the Royal Yacht Squadron's Dragon Class race at the Cowes Regatta. With him is his friend Uffa Fox, the yacht designer, who was crewing with Cyril Smith, unseen, a local yachtsman. The Duke was placed fifth out of 22 yachts that took part in the race.

The Duke of Edinburgh takes the reins of two shire horses as he leads other dignitaries through Battersea Park on a dray owned by Wandsworth-based brewery Young's during a visit following the completion of an £11 million restoration programme in the south London park. The photograph was taken on June 2, 2004.

Prime Minister Margaret Thatcher addresses the 32nd Commonwealth Parliamentary Conference in the Westminster Hall on September 25, 1986, watched by the Queen, as the Duke of Edinburgh listens.

Ideal for the palace! Prince Philip with his grandson Peter Phillips, being shown a burglar alarm which Peter had made for a classroom project at his Port Regis school in Dorset during the Queen and the Duke's visit on February 22, 1991.

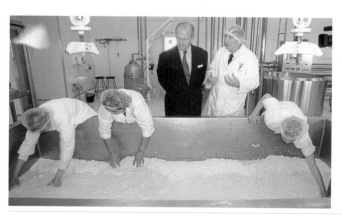

Prince Philip listens as Barry Lillywhite, Charles Sturt University's cheese factory manager, explains the process in Wagga Wagga, south-west of Sydney, Australia on March 21, 2000. The Duke refused to wear a sterile white laboratory coat or a cap and Mr Lillywhite said afterwards that the batch under production during the Duke's visit would be tested for contamination, but probably not offered for sale to the public.

A composite of four photos showing The Duke of Edinburgh unveiling a plaque at the end of his visit to Richmond Adult Community College in Richmond, south west London, on June 8, 2015 .

The Duke of Edinburgh and Christine Grahame, Deputy Presiding Officer, leave following the opening of the fifth session of the Scottish Parliament in Edinburgh on July 2, 2016.

January 1, 1929: Prince Philip of Greece is seen in the classroom at MacJannet American School in the Paris suburb of St Cloud.

This photograph of Princess Alice of Greece, wife of Prince Andrew and mother of the Duke of Edinburgh, is dated January 1, 1913.

Prince Andrew of Greece, the father of the Duke of Edinburgh – a photograph dated January 1, 1919.

Royal blood

Even before the Queen was born, it seemed to be written in the stars that she and Prince Philip would one day meet, fall in love and marry. Their paths were destined to cross as their shared lineage was deeply intertwined – the Duke, born Philip, prince of Greece and Denmark and the Queen, who is five years his junior, are both great-great-grandchildren of Queen Victoria.

Prince Philip is a direct descendant of Princess Alice, the third child of Queen Victoria; the Queen a direct descendant of Queen Victoria's eldest son, Prince Albert Edward (later King Edward VII).

Prince Philip of Greece, youngest child and only son of Prince Andrew of Greece and Princess Alice (of Battenberg), was born at the villa Mon Repos, the

summer retreat of the Greek royal family, on the island of Corfu on June 10, 1921.

His grandfather was a Prince of Denmark who became King of Greece, and the Duke's noble heritage extended even further as he was also related to kings of Prussia and emperors of Russia.

His early years were spent in France, but he went to live to England in 1928. He attended Gordonstoun boarding school in Scotland, after which he joined the Royal Navy and saw active service in the Second World War – see the following chapter.

The Duke renounced his Greek royal title in 1947 and became a naturalised British subject following his service in the Royal Navy.

December 1, 1939: a rare picture of Prince Philip of Greece at the public school of Gordonstoun in Scotland.

Young Prince Philip, second from left, is seen as a schoolboy at the MacJannet American School in St Cloud, France, in 1929 or 1930. His schoolmates, from left, are, Jacques de Bourbon; Teddy Culbert, son of a member of the US Foreign Service; and Alice Henderson, daughter of a South African doctor.

King Michael of Romania (right) rides with his cousin Prince Philip of Greece on the sands at Constanza on August 6, 1928.

Prince Philip of Greece (second from left), aged 12, takes part in an historical pageant at Gordonstoun school on August 8, 1933.

A prince becomes a king: Philip (centre left, kneeling) performs as King Melchior in a nativity play at Gordonstoun on December 12, 1938.

Prince Philip of Greece with the Junior Cricket Team (Prince Philip is tossing the ball in the air), at the public school of Gordonstoun on July 7, 1935.

Handsome, thoughtful and intelligent: three characteristics that shine from these black and white images of the Duke as a young man, and which no doubt endeared him to the young Princess Elizabeth.

The Duke of Edinburgh in his uniform as a Marshal of the Royal Air Force, one of his recent promotions, on March 17, 1953.

A military man

The Duke of Edinburgh has been photographed many times in a variety of uniforms, many of which were ceremonial. Even into his nineties he carried them off with aplomb, and has taken great pleasure in chatting to former services personnel over the years at Remembrance Day commemoration events.

The Duke is no stranger to the armed forces as he was on active service in the Royal Navy throughout the Second World War and had a proud military career from an early age. His first naval appointment, aged 18, was as a midshipman aboard battleship HMS *Ramillies*, which escorted the first contingents of the Allied Expeditionary Force from Australia to Egypt.

The Duke of Edinburgh was mentioned in despatches for his service in the Second World War. He joined another battleship, HMS *Valiant*, in the Mediterranean Fleet and was involved in engagements including, on March 21, 1941, the Battle of Cape Matapan (in Greek waters) against the Italian fleet.

For his work in control of the searchlights Prince Philip was mentioned in despatches. He was later awarded the Greek War Cross of Valour. Towards the end of the Second World War, Prince Philip served in the destroyer HMS *Whelp* in the Pacific, and was present in Tokyo Bay for the Japanese surrender on September 2, 1945.

From July 1951, the Duke of Edinburgh took up no more active naval appointments owing to Princess Elizabeth's increased royal responsibilities and her accession to the throne in 1953.

He was promoted to Admiral of the Fleet on January 15, 1953, and was appointed Lord High Admiral in 2011 on the occasion of his 90th birthday. He held 38 other military positions throughout the Commonwealth. His other British service appointments were Field Marshal of the Army and Marshal of the Royal Air Force.

The set of 17 medals he has worn comprised his service medals from the Second World War and various jubilee and coronation commemorative medals.

March 28, 1999: The Duke of Edinburgh, Colonel in Chief of the Army Cadet Force, meets cadets at Horse Guards Parade in London, as part of the launch of a brand new recruitment campaign designed to attract 13 to 18-year-old potential adult leaders to join the Army Cadet Force.

The Queen and the Duke of Edinburgh, who wears his Admiral's cocked hat, drive from Buckingham Palace to attend the dinner given by the Prime Minister at Lancaster House, St James, on June 5, 1953.

March 1, 1955: The Duke of Edinburgh has the leek straightened in his cap by Regimental Sergeant Major D J Griffiths during the St David's Day parade of the Welsh Guards, of which the Duke was colonel, at the Guards depot, Caterham, Surrey.

The Duke of Edinburgh in the uniform of Admiral of the Fleet visited the Nautical College, Pangbourne, Berkshire to present prizes and lay the foundation stone of a new building. This photograph was taken on July 27, 1953.

October 27, 1965: The Duke in uniform as Captain General of the Royal Marines pictured with his uncle, Admiral of the Fleet, Earl Mountbatten of Burma at the Royal Marines Barracks, Eastney, near Portsmouth.

The Duke of Edinburgh, in the uniform of a Marshal of the RAF with the riband and star of the Order of the Garter, in the carriage procession with Princess Muna Al Hussein, wife of King Hussein of Jordan, on July 19, 1966, as they arrived at Buckingham Palace. King Hussein and his wife were in Britain on a 10-day state visit.

The Duke talks to the oldest Chelsea pensioner, Sergeant Major Percy Talbot, 94, at Founder's Day at the Royal Hospital Chelsea, London, on June 8, 1978.

Captain General of the Royal Marines, the Duke of Edinburgh during the unveiling of the Royal Marines National Memorial in London on October 29, 2000. The service and rededication of the memorial was in honour of the 10,000 royal marines who fell in action in the 20th century.

The Duke salutes a parade of the Household Cavalry on June 5, 2004, ahead of the Trooping the Colour ceremony outside Buckingham Palace in London to mark the Queen's official birthday.

The Duke of Edinburgh shares an amusing anecdote with veterans during a visit to the Field of Remembrance at Westminster Abbey, London, on November 8, 2012.

Visiting a Cadet Training Centre in Surrey on July 12, 1978.

The Duke of Edinburgh salutes as he arrives at the laying up of the Colours of the Queen's Own Highlanders, to remember fallen soldiers from the regiment, at the Scottish National War Memorial in Crown Square at Edinburgh Castle on November 25, 2003.

Still meeting and greeting at 93... The Duke of Edinburgh speaks to families of soldiers of the 4th Battalion, The Royal Regiment of Scotland in Fallingbostel, Germany, on June 12, 2014.

October 17, 2007: Prince Philip, in his role as Master of Trinity House, waits to welcome Queen Elizabeth II aboard the new Trinity House Vessel THV *Galatea*, a lighthouse tender, which was moored on the Thames in London.

The Duke of Edinburgh, Captain General of the Royal Marines, during a visit to 1 Assault Group Royal Marines at HM Naval base Devonport in Plymouth on November 13, 2015.

Prince Philip of Greece, later to become the Duke of Edinburgh, acts as an usher, assisting Princess Elizabeth, right, and Princess Margaret Rose, with their coats as they arrive at Romsey Abbey, Hampshire, December 23, 1946, for the wedding of Patricia Mountbatten.

Love blossoms in wartime...

The young Princess Elizabeth first met her husband-to-be when she was just eight years old. They were both guests at the wedding of Philip's cousin, Princess Marina of Greece, to the Duke of Kent – an uncle of the princess – in 1934.

Elizabeth and Philip met again in 1939 and began to exchange letters during the Second World War. Prince Philip joined the Royal Navy in 1939 and after the war, in February 1947, became a naturalised British subject. Philip was required to choose a surname to continue his career in the Royal Navy and adopted Mountbatten, the name of his mother's British relatives.

The couple became secretly engaged in 1946, but the formal engagement of Princess Elizabeth and Lieutenant Philip Mountbatten, RN, was delayed until Elizabeth turned 21 in April 1947, being officially announced on July 9, 1947.

Philip, who had two stag parties the night before the wedding – the first at the Dorchester to which the press were invited and the second with his closest friends at the Belfry Club – was created Duke of Edinburgh by King George VI on marriage.

Princess Elizabeth's platinum and diamond engagement ring was made by the jewellers Philip Antrobus, using diamonds from a tiara belonging to Philip's mother.

July 10, 1947: The day after their engagement had been officially announced, Princess Elizabeth and Lieutenant Philip Mountbatten, RN, look happy and relaxed together at Buckingham Palace.

July 10, 1947: They pose for their first engagement pictures at Buckingham Palace.

Looking forward to a joyous future: the couple gaze into each other's eyes at Buckingham Palace on July 10, 1947 after announcing their engagement.

The couple arrive at Usher Hall, Edinburgh, Scotland on July 16, 1947. Princess Elizabeth was admitted to the Freedom of Edinburgh after attending a presentation party held by King George and Queen Elizabeth for 800 guests at the Palace of Holyroodhouse.

Princess Elizabeth is pictured dancing with Lieutenant Philip Mountbatten, her fiancé, at the Assembly Rooms, Edinburgh, on July 16, 1947, when a ball was held to welcome the Royal Family to Scotland.

Princess Elizabeth smiles as her fiancé signs the visiting book outside the town hall on July 18, 1947 in Galashiels, Scotland, during a tour of Scottish borders.

July 22, 1947: the newly engaged couple, pictured before the royal party left Greenock in the Royal Barge for a visit to the Home Fleet.

August 10, 1947: the newly betrothed couple are joined on the balcony by the King and Queen and Princess Margaret to acknowledge the cheering crowds.

On October 31, 1947, just days before their wedding, they were at Clydebank for the launching of the liner RMS *Caronia* and stopped by at the town hall to receive the town's wedding present – an electric sewing machine.

June 2, 1953: Queen Elizabeth II, Prince Charles, Princess Anne, the Duke of Edinburgh, the Queen Mother, and the Duke of Gloucester on the balcony of Buckingham Palace to view the flypast of the Royal Air Force after the coronation.

A fairy-tale wedding – and a coronation

Princess Elizabeth was aged 21 when she and Prince Philip were married at Westminster Abbey on November 20, 1947, in front of 2000 invited guests.

The ceremony was broadcast on the radio to 200 million listeners across the world, a joyful occasion after the stark, dark days of the Second World War.

Her wedding dress, designed by Norman Hartnell, was a duchesse satin bridal gown with motifs of star lilies and orange blossoms. As the wedding took place only a matter of months after the end of the war, Princess Elizabeth had to use ration coupons to obtain the material.

More than 2500 wedding presents arrived from around the world, and 10,000 telegrams of congratulations were sent to the happy couple.

After the ceremony they went to Buckingham Palace where they waved from the balcony to large crowds. They spent their wedding night in Broadlands, Hampshire, the home of Philip's uncle, Earl Mountbatten, and spent the rest of their honeymoon at Birkhall on the Balmoral Estate.

Just a few short years later, after the birth of their two eldest children, Charles and Anne, the couple were back at Westminster Abbey and again later seen together on the Buckingham Palace balcony after Princess Elizabeth was crowned Queen following the sudden death of her father in 1952 (see following chapter).

November 20, 1947: the couple leave Westminster Abbey after their wedding.

The couple with close relatives and bridesmaids in the Throne Room at Buckingham Palace immediately after the wedding ceremony. In the front row are (from left) Queen Mary (the King's mother), Princess Andrew of Greece (Duke of Edinburgh's mother), Prince William of Gloucester with fellow pageboy Prince Michael of Kent, King George VI and the Queen Mother. Back row, the bridesmaids are, from left: The Hon. Margaret Elphinstone, The Hon. Pamela Mountbatten, Lady Mary Cambridge, Princess Alexandra of Kent, Princess Margaret, Lady Caroline Montagu-Douglas-Scott, Lady Elizabeth Lambart and The Hon. Diana Bowes-Lyon.

The bride and bridegroom in a coach passing the Cenotaph on the way back to Buckingham Palace after their wedding.

The newlywed couple in an open landau on their way to Waterloo Station crossing Westminster Bridge.

Princess Elizabeth and the Duke of Edinburgh in procession to the west door of Westminster Abbey, London after their wedding.

The return from the abbey: the Duke of Edinburgh waves to the crowd as he rides in a coach with his bride.

Princess Elizabeth and her new husband at Buckingham Palace after their wedding ceremony.

Princess Elizabeth enjoys a stroll with her new husband on November 23, 1947. This was their first public appearance since their wedding three days earlier.

The Duke at the coronation at Westminster Abbey on June 2, 1953.

Newlyweds Princess Elizabeth and the Duke of Edinburgh at Buckingham Palace, being driven by carriage to the London Guildhall in June 1948 where the Duke was to receive the Freedom of the City of London.

Members of the royal family in the Royal Box at the Odeon Theatre, Leicester Square, London, on May 6, 1948 for the film premiere of the production Hamlet. Left to right are: Prince Philip, Duke of Edinburgh, Princess Elizabeth, King George VI, Queen Elizabeth, an unidentified man, and Princess Margaret.

Family tree, family ties

The royal couple, having married in November 1947, went on to have four children over a period spanning 16 years. Prince Charles was born almost a year to the day after his parents were wed, arriving on November 14, 1948. Two years later his only sister, Princess Anne, was born, and the senior siblings enjoyed taking part in photoshoots with their proud parents as they grew up together. Charles and Anne were presented with a brother when Prince Andrew was born in 1960, and the family was complete with the arrival four years later of Prince Edward.

Princes Charles may have merely fleeting memories of his maternal grandfather, as he had only just turned three years old when King George VI died in February 1952. Prince Philip broke the news of the King's sudden death to his wife, who was at the royal hunting lodge in Kenya when her father died overnight at Sandringham in Norfolk.

This meant that Princess Elizabeth, a 25-year-old mother of two young children, was immediately thrust headlong into the role of Queen. Her coronation was held at Westminster Abbey in June the following year and was televised to a worldwide audience of millions by the BBC.

Ever since, the Royal Family's movements have been followed closely by the media, most notably every December when they assemble at Sandringham for their festive celebration and traditional attendance at church on Christmas morning, when they are warmly greeted by well-wishers, whatever the weather.

As male head of the dynasty, The Duke of Edinburgh provided not only comfort to his wife but also to younger members of the family – namely his grandsons, William and Harry, after the death of their mother, Princess Diana.

It is reported that, when she died in 1997, the young men – then aged 15 and 12 respectively – did not want to walk behind the coffin, but Philip thought they would regret it later and told them: "If you like, I'll walk with you."

It seems that the Duke has earned a reputation for speaking his mind within his family as well as at social engagements. Prince William, now a father himself, is reported to have said in 2004 that his grandfather "will tell me something I don't want to hear and doesn't care if I get upset about it. He knows it is the right thing to say."

Princess Elizabeth pictured in the White Drawing Room at Buckingham Palace on September 5, 1947, with her husband to be, Lieutenant Philip Mountbatten and her sister, Princess Margaret.

Prince Charles sleeps in the arms of his mother, Princess Elizabeth, after his christening at Buckingham Palace on December 15, 1948. Looking on are, left, King George VI, The Duke of Edinburgh, and Queen Elizabeth.

These photographs of eight-month-old Prince Charles and his parents were the most informal ever taken of the baby prince and his youthful mother and father at the time. The pictures, taken on July 18, 1949, were from a film made for the British Newsreels Association in the grounds of Windlesham Moor, country home in Surrey of Princess Elizabeth and the Duke.

Princess Elizabeth, Prince Philip and their children Prince Charles and Princess Anne on the lawn at Clarence House, London, on August 8, 1951.

The royal couple are greeted on their arrival at London Airport on February 7, 1952. They cut short their official trip to Kenya and returned home following the death of King George VI. Prince Philip is talking to Earl Mountbatten of Burma, left.

Prince Charles, dangling his hand in an ornamental pond, The Queen, Princess Margaret, The Duke of Edinburgh, King George VI, Princess Elizabeth and Princess Anne, in a pram, on holiday at Balmoral on August 21, 1951.

The Queen and the Duke of Edinburgh and their children, Princess Anne, left, and Prince Charles at Balmoral Castle on January 21, 1953.

June 7, 1954: Princess Margaret smiles as she presents the Duke of Sutherland Cup to her brother-in-law, the Duke of Edinburgh, after the Cowdray Park team had beaten the Greyhounds in the final at the Polo tournament at Cowdray Park, Midhurst, Sussex.

The Queen, Prince Charles, Prince Edward, Prince Andrew and Princess Anne listening to the Duke of Edinburgh on a bridge in the grounds of Frogmore, Windsor, on April 21, 1968.

Prince Charles points something out to his father, the Duke of Edinburgh, at Heathrow Airport on October 15, 1956. Prince Charles was going with the Queen and Princess Anne to say goodbye to the Duke, who was leaving on a three-month world tour.

June 2, 1959, saw the Queen and Duke of Edinburgh at Windsor joined by Sugar, one of the royal corgis.

The Duke receives a polo stick from his son Prince Edward, aged seven, at Windsor Great Park during a polo match in May 1971.

The Duke and his second-born son, Prince Andrew, alight from their railway carriage at Liverpool Street Station, London, on return from Sandringham with the Queen and Prince Edward on January 27, 1965.

October 31, 1972: The Queen, the Duke of Edinburgh and their son Prince Andrew visit the kennels at Balmoral.

Prince Edward, The Earl of Wessex, his father the Duke of Edinburgh and the Countess of Wessex at a reception ahead of the Duke of Edinburgh Award garden party, at Buckingham Palace, London, on May 16, 2016.

September 6, 1997: the funeral of Diana, Princess of Wales. The Duke of Edinburgh, Prince William, Earl Spencer, Prince Harry and the Prince of Wales follow the coffin of Diana, Princess of Wales, to Westminster Abbey for her funeral service.

The Prince of Wales, Duke of Edinburgh and Queen Elizabeth the Queen Mother leave St George's Chapel in the precincts of Windsor Castle on June 10, 2001, after a service of thanksgiving. Fifty royals were at Windsor to celebrate the Duke of Edinburgh's 80th birthday.

The Queen and the Duke of Edinburgh enjoy an impromptu song by the Beverley Sisters, (from left) Babs, Joy and Teddie, at the Broadway Theatre in Catford, south-east London where the veteran entertainers were restaging a show which they first performed in 1952 to celebrate the Queen's Golden Jubilee visit to South London. The picture was taken on July 4, 2002.

Celebrity circles

Over the decades, thousands of people from all walks of life have shared a few words and the occasional joke with the Duke of Edinburgh.

Many were off-the-cuff remarks and conversations as the Duke and the Queen attended official events, and time and again the Duke demonstrated an innate ability to put people at their ease during a wide variety of public engagements. Pop stars, actors, musicians, comedians and a host of other entertainers were introduced to the Duke, with many celebrities attending events connected with the Duke of Edinburgh's Award (see following chapter).

Despite their own celebrity status, these household names may well have felt overawed at the thought of meeting senior members of the Royal Family, especially in the 1960s and 1970s when more and more British families were buying televisions and every move of the rich and famous could be captured and replayed on-screen in front of millions. As black and white images turned to high-definition colour with frequent technological advances, the Duke continued his relaxed meet-and-greet style, managing to put people at their ease and leaving them with memories to savour.

Television soap operas including EastEnders and Coronation Street played host to the Duke on occasion – both shows feature a traditional British 'local', and the Duke obviously enjoyed meeting some of the queens and kings of these long-running series before heading back to Buckingham Palace. Who knows what conversations he had with the Queen as he relayed details of his entertaining solo engagements to his wife later in the day or over breakfast!

In the following pages we look back down the years at some of the many well known and loved entertainers who graced the small screen, the stage and the cinematic screen and who engaged in conversation with Prince Philip, often as part of their commitment to charitable causes.

American singer Eartha Kitt is presented to the Duke of Edinburgh after the Royal Variety Performance at the Coliseum, London, on November 3, 1958.

April 14, 1955: the Queen and the Duke of Edinburgh meet singer Alma Cogan and show presenter Jack Hylton after the Royal Variety Performance at the Opera House, Blackpool, Lancashire.

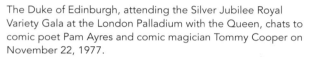

The Duke of Edinburgh, attending the Silver Jubilee Royal Variety Gala at the London Palladium with the Queen, chats to comic poet Pam Ayres and comic magician Tommy Cooper on November 22, 1977.

American singer and actor Bing Crosby, who was appearing in a series of London charity concerts, at Buckingham Palace when he attended a small drinks party given in his honour by the Duke of Edinburgh on July 1, 1976. From left are: Mary Francis (Bing's daughter), American singer and actress Rosemary Clooney, the Duke of Edinburgh, Bing Crosby and his son Harry.

The Duke of Edinburgh talking with Goon comedian Spike Milligan, one of the guests at a Foyles lunch given in the Duke's honour at the Dorchester Hotel, Park Lane, London on November 2, 1978. It was to celebrate the publication of The Environmental Revolution, a collection of the Duke's speeches on the environment.

The Duke of Edinburgh talking to actress Pat Phoenix on May 5, 1982 when he and the Queen visited the newly built outdoor location in Manchester for Granada Television's Coronation Street. Miss Phoenix played Elsie Tanner in the serial, the longest running on British television.

May 11, 1982: an air of mime during the Variety Club luncheon at the London Hilton hotel for the Outward Bound Trust, seemingly enacted by Royal Patron, the Duke of Edinburgh and entertainer Lionel Blair of the Give Us A Clue TV mime show. Watching is sports commentator Dickie Davies while actor Sir John Mills is partially hidden from view.

The Duke of Edinburgh uses burly comedian Les Dawson as a punch bag during the National Sponsored Sports Luncheon at Grosvenor House Hotel, London, on April 26, 1983. The event was organised by the Variety Club of Great Britain.

The Duke of Edinburgh and Terry Wogan, as viewers of BBC TV's Wogan chat show saw them on July 9, 1986.

The Duke was in an animated mood at the Grosvenor House Hotel, chatting to boxers Frank Bruno (left) and Floyd Patterson (centre), while attending the National Sponsored Sports Luncheon organised by the Variety Club of Great Britain on April 26, 1983.

May 8, 1985, saw the Duke of Edinburgh at the National Sponsored Sports luncheon, organised by The Variety Club of Great Britain, at the Cafe Royal, London. The Duke is pictured enjoying chatting with strongman Geoff Capes and footballer Charlie Nicholas.

April 3, 1998, meeting violinist Vanessa Mae following a concert at Buckingham Palace after an official dinner for Asia-European leaders.

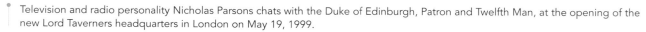

Television and radio personality Nicholas Parsons chats with the Duke of Edinburgh, Patron and Twelfth Man, at the opening of the new Lord Taverners headquarters in London on May 19, 1999.

The Duke chats with TV gardener Alan Titchmarsh and wife during a garden party hosted by the Duke at Buckingham Palace in July 1999.

May 2001: Meeting singer Dame Shirley Bassey at the Royal Albert Hall in London. The Prince was attending a celebration to mark the 45th anniversary of the Duke of Edinburgh's Award and his own 80th birthday.

November 28, 2001 The Duke of Edinburgh with EastEnders' actor Wendy Richard, who played Pauline Fowler in the BBC soap, during his visit to the programme's set in Elstree.

Family business! The Duke meets EastEnders actor Steve McFadden, who plays Phil Mitchell in the BBC soap, during his visit to Elstree.

The Duke of Edinburgh meets actress Anna Friel at the Duke of Edinburgh's Award garden party, at Buckingham Palace, London, on May 16, 2016.

The Duke speaks with Ronan Keating and his wife Storm at the Duke of Edinburgh's Award garden party, at Buckingham Palace, London, on May 16, 2016.

Bridging the generation gap – Prince Philip meets Duke of Edinburgh Award recipients.

Supporting young people

Sixty years of the Duke of Edinburgh's Award Scheme and International Award have resulted in millions of young people from more than 90 countries growing their skills and knowledge.

The Duke founded the award projects in 1956 to introduce young people to new experiences, including physical, skills-based and community challenges.

The International Award was founded in conjunction with German educationalist Kurt Hahn as both he and the Duke were concerned that young people's development was lacking in certain key areas. They resolved to create a programme that would be a "do-it-yourself kit in the art of civilised living".

The subsequent spread of the award across the globe –

in 2014 alone, more than 1.1 million young people took part in 141 countries and territories, equipping them with skills for life – is testament to the universal appeal of the programme, and the vision of its founder.

However, even the Duke admitted that this had taken him by surprise: "When the first trial of the award was launched in 1956, no one had any idea quite what would happen. In the event it was an instant success, and the award has been growing and expanding worldwide ever since."

The Duke of Edinburgh remained committed to the award since its birth six decades ago and continued his involvement, particularly in recognising the achievements of award participants and the adults who support them in reaching their goals.

The Duke of Edinburgh and Jane Torvill at the Duke of Edinburgh Award garden party, at Buckingham Palace, London, on May 16, 2016.

July 31, 1975: Prince Philip talks with 19-year-old Kim Turner, of London, in the quadrangle of Buckingham Palace before she set off with eight other riders – several of them Duke of Edinburgh Gold Award winners – for a sponsored cycle ride to Windsor Castle to start off the award scheme's fund-raising event of 1975.

It's the way he tells them! The Duke enjoys a joke with comedian Frank Carson (right) during a Variety Club of Great Britain luncheon, held at London's Inn on the Park Hotel on November 26, 1985, in aid of the Duke of Edinburgh's Award Scheme. Centre is the Chief Barker John Ratcliffe.

Film star Brooke Shields with British-born veteran Hollywood comedian Bob Hope, British actor Ben Kingsley and the Duke of Edinburgh at the Lyric Theatre, Shaftesbury Avenue, London, for the Bob Hope 82nd Birthday Show. The show, on May 15, 1985, was in aid of the Duke of Edinburgh's Award Scheme.

July 2003, the Duke attends The Duke of Edinburgh Gold Award presentation Ceremony at the Palace of Holyroodhouse, Edinburgh.

October 10, 2013: The Duke speaks with a group of young people during a reception for his Duke of Edinburgh Award (DOE) programme at James's Palace, London.

Actor Benedict Cumberbatch shakes hands with the Duke of Edinburgh during a DofE Gold Award Presentation at St James's Palace, London, on March 19, 2014. Photo courtesy The Duke of Edinburgh's Award / Tempest Photography

The Duke meets athlete Hannah Cockroft at a reception ahead of the Duke of Edinburgh Award garden party, at Buckingham Palace, London, on May 16, 2016.

The Duke chats with Joanna Lumley during a gala evening marking the 60th anniversary of The Duke of Edinburgh's Award, at Stoke Park, Stoke Poges, Buckinghamshire, on June 9, 2016.

Dame Judi Dench shares a joke with the Prince during the Stoke Park gala evening.

The Duke shakes hands with Arsenal Football Club manager Arsene Wenger on the pitch as he officially opens the Emirates Stadium in north London on October 26, 2006.

Work, rest and play

Sometimes work, rest and play can go hand in hand. The Duke has the ability to turn his own much-shaken hand to making his duties a fun and memorable event for people, for pets, and even for wildlife!

A classic example of his quick wit was in October 2006, when he officially opened the new Emirates Stadium, home of Arsenal Football Club. It had been intended that the Queen would open the stadium as well, but she suffered a back injury and was unable to attend on the day. Prince Philip quipped: "Well, you may not have my wife, but you've got the second-

most experienced plaque unveiler in the world." As a result of the change of plan, the Queen extended to the club the honour of inviting the chairman, manager and first team to join her for afternoon tea at Buckingham Palace in February 2007 – the first football club ever to be invited to the palace for such an event.

Over the years, as can be seen from this selection of engaging images, the Duke made four-legged as well as two-legged friends in his role supporting the Queen, while carrying off a host of official and social engagements with aplomb.

The Duke took turns batting and bowling during a 12-a-side cricket match between the Duke of Edinburgh and the Duke of Norfolk on August 2, 1953. Prince Philip's team was mainly made up of former England cricketers and Norfolk's consisted mainly of Sussex players.

The dress dummy brought a quip from Prince Philip and a laugh in response from mini-skirted dress design student Pat Willis, 17, of Oldham during the Duke's tour of the Salford, Lancashire, Technical College, on June 15, 1967. He was in Lancashire to be installed as Chancellor of Salford University and also to attend the opening of the Technical College.

Prince Philip walks out on to the pitch at Dean Park, Bournemouth, on September 20, 1949 for the match between the Duke's County Players Team and Hampshire in a match to aid the National Playing Fields Association.

A foaming glass of beer is accepted by the Duke of Edinburgh from a workman at the site of the City and Guilds of London Institute's new London headquarters in Portland Place, London, where the Duke had just laid the foundation stone on February 18, 1958.

Refreshment for the Duke of Edinburgh at Cowdray Park, Midhurst, when the Duke's team Windsor Park narrowly lost to The Centaurs, seven goals to eight, on July 4, 1965.

The Duke of Edinburgh visiting the Hudson's Bay Company post at Whitehorse, Yukon, Canada, on August 16, 1954.

The Duke waves to the crowd waiting for him as he leaves the Harrow Club in Bard Road, Notting Hill, London, on May 25, 1959. The club, entirely supported by the Harrow School, was one of those visited by the Duke, who is patron of the London Federation of Boys' Clubs.

The Duke of Edinburgh, President of the British National Appeal and International Trustee of the World Wildlife Fund, chatting to Eva Rueber-Staier, who won the Miss World title for Austria in 1969, but was World Wildlife Fund's Wildlife Girl when this photograph was taken in July 1971. They were attending the 10th anniversary ball at Hurlingham Club, Fulham, of World Wildlife.

Prince Philip cuts a candlelit birthday cake presented to him on his 45th birthday at Manchester Town Hall on June 10, 1966. On the right is the Lord Mayor of Manchester, Alderman Mrs Nellie Beer. The Duke was attending the third biennial meeting of the General Council of his Award Scheme.

The Duke of Edinburgh meets Belinda Vinns (left) and Amanda Brooks, both seven and from Chingford, London, at the trampoline when he opened the Picketts Lock Centre at Edmonton, London, on June 13, 1973. It was claimed to be the biggest recreation, sports and leisure complex in the UK.

Visitors' favourite Guy the Gorilla peers from his cage at the Duke of Edinburgh, who visited London Zoo on May 4, 1976. The Duke's visit was part of the Thames Television Today programme.

Sandy, the dog who had a part in the then-new musical Annie, steps up to meet the Duke of Edinburgh when he went backstage at the Victoria Palace Theatre in London after attending a gala performance of the show on May 3, 1978. Amused by Sandy's antics is Andrea McArdle, who was playing the title role in the musical.

March 28, 1980: The Duke of Edinburgh, Chancellor of Cambridge University, visiting the Cambridge crew for the Boat Race. He is surrounded by a group of St Trinians 'schoolgirls', who were there to publicise their new film Wildcats of St Trinians.

The Duke of Edinburgh at the controls of a Boeing 757 airliner during a one and a half hour demonstration flight near Seattle on April 20, 1982.

Holding a family pet, the Duke of Edinburgh leaves the Hawker Siddeley Andover of The Queen's Flight – piloted by his son, the Prince of Wales – on arrival at Aberdeen Airport en route to a Highland holiday at Balmoral, Deeside, on August 16, 1982.

Laughter all round as schoolgirl Rachel Kennedy (seated right), too shy to give her posy to the Queen as planned, hands it instead to the Duke of Edinburgh in Great Wymondley during the royal visit to Hertfordshire on July 8, 1982.

November 20, 1983. The Duke, President of the International Wildlife Fund, sits atop an elephant while visiting the Kanha Game Reserve during his 10-day tour of India with the Queen.

July 1985: The Duke of Edinburgh nimbly jumps ashore from the Royal Forth Yacht Club vessel *Royal Forth* after a tour of Granton Harbour, Edinburgh.

Patron of the British Heart Foundation, the Duke of Edinburgh, in the grounds of Buckingham Palace on May 29, 1985, cutting a heart-shaped cake to give a royal send-off to Heart Week '85. He is watched by Lord Soames (behind the Duke) and other former heart patients. The group, living proof of the week's theme Research Saves Lives, are (from left) Tania Didwell, 20 months and in the arms of her father, Peter Rawley, 51, Ann Tooth, 50, Lindsay Stickland, 30, Linda Rooney, 30, and at the front is Katherine Bradley, four, and Elliot Fleisher, eight.

Visiting US President George Bush inspecting the Guard of
Honour in the Quadrangle at Buckingham Palace with the Duke
of Edinburgh on June 1, 1989. President Bush and his wife
Barbara were the Queen and the Duke's lunch guests.

The Duke, accompanied by Lord Derby, (right) and David Ross,
manager of Knowles Safari Park, meet Chota, the oldest elephant
in the herd at the North West safari park, on July 8, 2000.

The Duke rides a mini motorbike around the Royal
Windsor Horse Show, on his way to watch his friend
Lady Romsey compete in the carriage driving
competition on May 16, 2002.

Hello, old stick! The Duke meets walking-stick maker David Duke (left) from Northbrook near Kirtlington, Oxfordshire, at the Royal Show, Stoneleigh, Warwickshire, on July 3, 2002.

It's good for you! The Duke offers a pint of beer to Ambassador the dray horse at the Bass Brewery Museum during the Golden Jubilee visit by himself and the Queen to Burton on Trent on July 3, 2002.

December 5, 2003: the Duke tours the Commonwealth People's Forum in Abuja, Nigeria, on the opening day of the Commonwealth Heads of Governments Meeting.

The Duke of Edinburgh meets Buddhist Monk Reverend Nagase at the Peace Pagoda in Battersea Park during a visit following the completion of a £11 million restoration programme in the south London park on June 2, 2004.

October 8, 2013 was a key date in the diary for residents of the Green Lane View assisted living residence, when the Duke paid an official visit to the St Michael's Care Complex in Aylsham, Norfolk, providing care for the elderly.

Meeting the England cricket team on the second day of the Lords Test Match, London, on July 17, 2009.

Seventy years of sartorial splendour

The Duke of Edinburgh, like many gentlemen of his era, has always looked smart and well turned out, whether accompanying the Queen or attending events in his own right. His lithe, athletic figure and imposing stature led to him being ranked 12th in a list of Britain's best-dressed men at the age of 94 by GQ magazine – featuring higher on the list than his grandson Prince Harry and his son Prince Charles.

In uniform – he has held a number of honorary military positions in Australia, Canada and New Zealand, and also held the title of Field Marshal of the British Army from 1953 (see Chapter 3) – the Duke always appeared immaculate and chivalrous. But in the many thousands of civic and public engagements he has undertaken over several decades, the dapper Duke's understated style was mostly fashioned for him by his long-time tailor, John Kent.

Mr Kent said of the Duke: "You have to be able to judge the moment, as with all customers. If he has a lot on, an important meeting, then you act accordingly. But if he is relaxed and has time, he has a wonderful sense of humour." John Kent's services as tailor to the Duke have been recognised with the Royal Warrant which he still holds, and he has been a guest at parties at Windsor Castle and Buckingham Palace.

The Scottish knitwear firm Lyle & Scott is also a Royal Warrant holder. From 1956 on, the Duke's shoes have been made by John Lobb Ltd, while his hats were produced by James Lock & Co, both of Jermyn Street.

Daks or Barbour made his favoured coats, his silk ties came from the French company Hermes, while his boots were from Hunter. Kinloch Anderson in Edinburgh made his kilts. Davies & Son covered the Duke's military requirements and his naval dress was tailored by Gieves & Hawkes. All Warrant Holders – for ceremonial robes, kilts, waterproofs, hats, shoes, knitwear, boots, buttons and hairdressing and so on – must have previously chalked up five years' service to attain a Warrant, and by definition they have to represent quality and reliability.

Ede & Ravenscroft, one of the oldest of companies holding a Royal Warrant, dating back to 1689, carried out the role of robe maker to the Duke.

Prince Philip has surely been aware that the eyes of the world would usually be on his wife, or other prominent female royals, with fashion editors and the public in general observing and commenting on the ladies' fashion sense and colour choices.

But the straight-backed senior royal would have been determined not to let down his family in the sartorial stakes and would have always aimed to look his best at official and public engagements, both at home and on the world stage.

Although being a leading light in the world of men's fashion, it seems he was not averse to recycling some of his outfits. It's said that in 2008 he asked his tailor to alter a pair of trousers he first wore more than half a century beforehand, and due to being able to keep his trim figure despite the many banquets he has attended over the years, this could be done.

But at times when tradition, respect or health and safety rules dictated, the stylish Duke had to forego his usual smart suit or warm overcoat to don something more practical or suitable to the occasion. Here we feature a selection of some of the Duke's finest outfits, and one or two items that perhaps he would have preferred not to have been asked to wear.

The Duke looks relaxed yet smart as he circulates among guests at the Garden Party at Buckingham Palace July 15, 2003.

The Duke of Edinburgh visiting the Royal Marines Eastney Barracks, Portsmouth on July 16, 1953 accompanied by Lieutenant-General John Westall. Both men wore Royal Marines officers' mess dress.

A smiling Duke of Edinburgh, wearing the uniform of Admiral of the Fleet, is welcomed to Paris at the Elysee Palace by the French President Rene Coty on June 22, 1954.

The Duke is treated to an impromptu concert by miners during his visit to the Fernhill Colliery in the Rhondda Valley on April 29, 1955.

May 1996, competing in the Windsor Horse Show.

Looking sprightly in a smart jacket and bowler hat, May 1993.

Prince Philip, President of the English Speaking Union, greets Sir Basil Smallpeice, chairman, at the Hilton Hotel, London, on November 30, 1966. They were attending the first annual Churchill Memorial Banquet of the English Speaking Union, held on the 92nd anniversary of Sir Winston Churchill's birth.

August 2002 sees the Duke at Balmoral in a kilt.

December 2003. The Duke leaves church on the Sandringham Estate following a Sunday service. The Queen, who had undergone an operation on her knee, did not attend the service.

The Duke of Edinburgh at the Royal International Air Tattoo at Fairford in Gloucestershire, July 2003.

The Duke of Edinburgh wears a headscarf during a visit to Gurdwara Sri Guru Singh Sabha (the Sikh Temple) in Hounslow, west London, on October 15, 2004. The royal couple opened a £2.5 million phase of development.

April 1, 2004: The Duke during his visit with the Queen to Harrow, west London, to celebrate the 50th anniversary of its royal charter.

The Duke wears a hard hat bearing his title as he tours the new Baglan Power Station in Port Talbot, South Wales, on October 28, 2004.

Prince Philip attends the Thistle Service for the installation of his grandson Prince William, Earl of Strathearn, as a Knight of the Thistle at St Giles Cathedral, Edinburgh on July 5, 2012.

Quips and quotes

Over the years, the Duke of Edinburgh quipped and tripped his way through a variety of public engagements and meetings with people of many nations.

On occasion, he certainly seems to have spoken before engaging his brain, bringing into focus one of his many famous quotes: "Dontopedology is the science of opening your mouth and putting your foot in it."

However, although many people who meet her seem to be in awe of the Queen, and are aware of the protocol that dictates that everyone must wait for the Queen to address them, there often seemed to be a less formal air and a more relaxed atmosphere when the Duke of Edinburgh started to chat with people at public engagements.

Here is a selection of some of his most well publicised and sometimes politically incorrect comments and observations:

1967
When asked if he would like to visit the Soviet Union, he replied: "I would like to go to Russia very much, although the bastards murdered half my family."

1969
The Duke said to Tom Jones after his Royal Variety Performance: "What do you gargle with, pebbles?" He later added: "It is very difficult at all to see how it is possible to become immensely valuable by singing what I think are the most hideous songs."

On the Royal Family's finances: "We go into the red next year. I shall probably have to give up polo."

1976
On a tour of Canada: "We don't come here for our health. We can think of other ways of enjoying ourselves."

1986
He told a World Wildlife Fund meeting that "if it has got four legs and it is not a chair, if it has got two wings and flies but is not an aeroplane and if it swims and it is not a submarine, the Cantonese will eat it."

While on an official visit to China, he told a group of British exchange students living in the city of Xian: "If you stay here much longer you'll all be slitty-eyed." His thoughts on Beijing: "Ghastly."

1994
"Aren't most of you descended from pirates?" he asked an islander in the Cayman Islands.

1995
He asked a Scottish driving instructor in Oban: "How do you keep the natives off the booze long enough to pass the test?"

1998
The Duke asked a British student who had been trekking in Papua New Guinea: "You managed not to get eaten then?"

2001
To Elton John: "Oh it's you that owns that ghastly car is it? We often see it when driving to Windsor Castle."

2002
While touring a factory near Edinburgh he said a fuse box was so crude it "looked as though it had been put in by an Indian".

To Australian Aborigines during a visit to Australia with the Queen he asked: "Do you still throw spears at each other?"

2009
Said to black dance troupe Diversity at the Royal Variety Performance: "Are you all one family?"

To a young fashion designer at Buckingham Palace he said: "You didn't design your beard too well, did you? You really must try better with your beard."

On asking a female Sea Cadet what she did for a living, and being told that she worked in a nightclub (as a barmaid), the Duke asked: "Is it a strip club?" Observing her surprise, he dismissed the suggestion, saying that it was "probably too cold for that anyway".

What on earth was that? The Duke of Edinburgh reacts to a blast from the ship's foghorn as he leaves after a visit to the QE2 in Southampton docks on November 11, 2008.

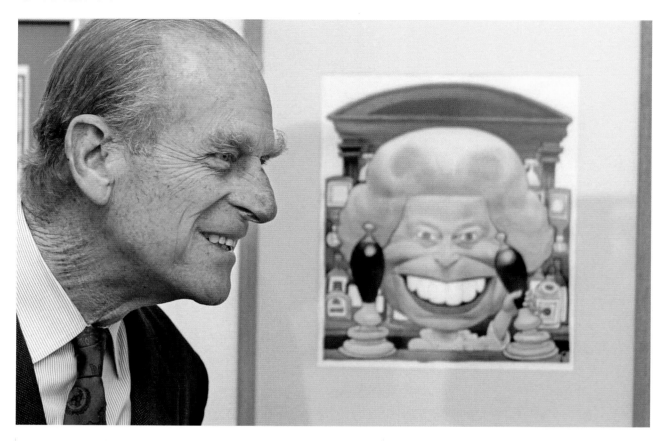

Queen of pubs: The Duke looks at a cartoon of his wife behind the bar in the Old Vic pub from TV show Eastenders drawn by Trogg for the Golden Jubilee. The Duke was on a visit to the Cartoon Art Trust's Kings and Queens exhibition at the Mall Galleries, London, of which he is a patron, in December 2002.

Half a gallon: The Duke enquires about a four-pint jug after he had pulled a pint at the Wadworth Brewery at Devizes, Wiltshire, on May 4, 2004.

Really? Prince Philip
at a reception held
at Windsor Castle
for the Bloomsbury
Qatar Foundation
Publishing Project
on April 6, 2010.

Oops! The Duke of Edinburgh with Claire Murdoch, chief executive of the Central and North West London NHS Trust during a visit to the Margaret Pyke Centre on May 21, 2014, which provides basic and specialist sexual reproductive healthcare in London, where he unveiled a plaque and observed a medical training procedure.

Straight from the horse's mouth: The expression on the Duke's face says it all. He was impersonating how his horse was biting his bit in an explanation to the judge during the World FEI Four-in-Hand Driving Championship at the Silver Ring racecourse at Ascot, Berkshire, on August 13, 1986.

The Duke famously proclaimed:

"British women can't cook."

"YOU have mosquitos. I have the Press."
To the matron of a hospital in the Caribbean.

"If it doesn't fart or eat hay then she isn't interested..."
Speaking about his daughter, Princess Anne, and her love of horses.

"Can you tell the difference between them?"
The Duke's question after President Barack Obama said he met with the leaders of the UK, China and Russia.

"The problem with London is the tourists. They cause the congestion. If we could just stop the tourism, we could stop the congestion."
On London traffic.

"Well, you'll never fly in it, you're too fat to be an astronaut."
To a 13-year-old while visiting a space shuttle.

"You look like you're ready for bed!"
To the President of Nigeria, dressed in traditional robes.

"I must confess that I am interested in leisure in the same way that a poor man is interested in money."

"The art of being a good guest is to know when to leave."

"All money nowadays seems to be produced with a natural homing instinct for the Treasury."

The couple sit with hands clasped in their laps as they leave the Temple Bar entrance to the heart of London on May 19, 1954 in an open carriage en route to Mansion House to be the luncheon guests of London's Lord Mayor Sir Noel Bowater. The luncheon followed the traditional sword-touching ceremony at Temple Bar in which the Queen's request to enter the city was granted and was part of her welcome home celebration.

Side by side

Although the Queen and the Duke of Edinburgh have fulfilled numerous engagements across the world separately, it has always brought great joy to followers of the Royal Family to see the couple side by side. As is plainly visible in many of the following photographs, even after more than 70 years as a couple there remains an unbreakable bond between them.

While many marriages have fallen by the wayside, not least within their own family, the love between the Queen and her prince has withstood the test of time, transcending all manner of political, social, governmental and international transitions, disagreements and upheavals. Maintaining her innate dignity after more than 60 years on the throne, the gracious Queen remains the focal figure within the spectrum of public engagements that she and her husband attend together.

They present themselves as a couple living in love and harmony – not for them the often-seen public squabbles of some celebrity pairings that quickly wither and fade under the glare of the spotlight or the camera lens. Here we offer a selection of images of the royal couple – some long forgotten, others much more recent and memorable – attending engagements together. A smile here, a tender glance there, a gentle tilting of the head… all signifying the deep-seated affection shared during this most extraordinary of partnerships.

A yellow buttonhole from the Prince as the couple arrive at Royal Ascot in June 1998.

February 1, 1956:
the couple at a
State dinner in
Lagos, Nigeria.

March 3, 1948: Princess Elizabeth and her husband study a chart showing New Zealand barque *Pamir* at Shadwell Basin, London.

Princess Elizabeth and the Duke of Edinburgh walking along the racecourse at Epsom, on June 5, 1948, before the start of the Derby.

Princess Elizabeth and her husband, the Duke of Edinburgh, leave the British Embassy in Paris on May 16, 1948 en route to the British Embassy church for services.

Starting out on the path of married life: The Duke of Edinburgh and his wife, then Princess Elizabeth, leave the Guildhall, where he received the Freedom of the City of London on June 8, 1948.

Princess Elizabeth in Rome as she presents a souvenir medal to her husband after his polo team The Optimist lost 9-4 in Italy on April 22, 1951. The winning team received the cups while the losers received the medals.

April 21, 1950: this image shows Princess Elizabeth with the Duke of Edinburgh at Earl Mountbatten Villa in Malta where she was staying and where she celebrated her 24th birthday.

Princess Elizabeth and the Duke of Edinburgh in an open Cadillac during their drive through Toronto, Canada, on October 16, 1951.

The Princess looks elegant and composed as she visits Windsor, Ontario, on October 25, 1951, with her husband by her side.

Queen Elizabeth II, wearing black, and a white hat, drives in an open carriage from the Golden Gates at Ascot Racecourse, Berkshire, on the afternoon of June 18, 1952, with the Duke of Edinburgh. This was the second day of the Royal Ascot meeting, an event which has always proved popular with the royal couple.

November 4, 1951: the couple stepped into a blustering snow storm which had blanketed the rolling Laurentian hills when they left church services at the Trinity Anglican Church in Ste. Agathe Des Monts, Quebec, Canada.

November 4, 1952: Queen Elizabeth II, accompanied by the Duke of Edinburgh, opened Parliament for the first time in her reign.

Happy and glorious: this picture, taken on November 4, 1952, shows the Queen and the Duke of Edinburgh on the balcony at Buckingham Palace in the afternoon after the State Opening of Parliament.

An intimate moment as Queen Elizabeth II and the Duke of Edinburgh attending a gala performance of Bertram Mills Circus at Olympia, London, on December 18, 1952.

February 18, 1955: the Shah of Persia with his wife Queen Soraya at Buckingham Palace, London, with the Queen, the Duke of Edinburgh, Prince Charles and Princess Anne, during a short visit to Britain.

May 2, 1953: the Queen presents the FA Cup to the winning captain, Blackpool's Harry Johnston, watched by the Duke of Edinburgh and FA chairman Stanley Rous.

February 3, 1954: the Queen and the Duke step ashore from a pontoon at Farm Cove, Sydney, to begin their tour of Australia.

June 25, 1955: the Queen and the Duke pause among the grey headstones to pay tribute in the Vestre Gravlund, the Western Cemetery, in Oslo, where 102 war dead are buried, mostly members of the British and Canadian Royal Air Forces. Between the royal couple is Mr J C Aird, British Consul in Oslo, who administers the cemetery.

The Queen, the Duke of Edinburgh and the Prince of Wales visiting Peter Scott (right) at the Severn Wildfowl Trust at Slimbridge in Gloucestershire. The photograph is dated April 22, 1961.

September 8, 1960: making a happy group on the lawns at Balmoral are the Queen, the Duke of Edinburgh and their three children Princess Anne, Prince Charles and baby Prince Andrew, who is perched on his father's knees.

Royals, including the Queen Mother, gather as President Julius Nyerere of Tanzania entertains the Queen and the Duke of Edinburgh with a banquet at Claridge's Hotel on November 20, 1975.

November 22, 1988: The Duke of Edinburgh helps his wife to alight from the new £120,000 Australia State Coach, Australia's bicentennial gift, at the Houses of Parliament as they arrive for the State Opening.

The Queen and the Duke of Edinburgh on the new Humber Bridge on July 17, 1981, after the Queen had declared the new bridge formally open. It actually opened to traffic 22 days earlier. The Queen and Duke then drove across the £91 million structure, the world's longest suspension bridge at the time, from the Hull side to the Grimsby side.

An undated image of the Queen and Prince Philip walking to the House of Lords before the Queen's speech.

Looking relaxed and happy, the couple enjoy a tribute to celebrate the 40th anniversary of the Queen's accession at the Fountain Court Palace on July 8, 1992.

Isn't this amazing? The Queen and the Duke on the Great Wall of China at the Bedaling Pass, 50 miles north-west of Beijing, on the third day of their State Visit to the country on October 14, 1986.

May 5, 1995: The Queen, flanked by the Prince of Wales and the Duke of Edinburgh, addresses both Houses of Parliament to mark the 50th anniversary of the end of the Second World War, at Westminster Hall in London.

May 6, 1994: Queen Elizabeth II and the Duke of Edinburgh travelling on the new Eurostar train, with politicians including the Prime Minister at that time, John Major, in seats behind.

June 17, 1996: The Queen and the Duke of Edinburgh arrive for the Garter ceremony at St George's Chapel in Windsor Castle.

November 19, 1997: The Queen and Duke of Edinburgh smile as they arrive at the Guildhall, for a lunch to celebrate their golden wedding anniversary.

Well, that's lunch sorted, then! All smiles as the Queen and the Duke of Edinburgh are presented with a tray of hot cross buns by a local baker, during a walkabout outside the Guildhall in Portsmouth on April 9, 1998.

Another joyful moment as The Queen and Duke of Edinburgh meet guests, all couples celebrating 50 years of marriage, at a special golden wedding anniversary Buckingham Palace garden party on July 15, 1997.

Colour reigns as the Queen and the Duke of Edinburgh attend day four of Royal Ascot 2016 at Ascot Racecourse on June 17.

The smartly attired couple prepare for an enjoyable few hours on day one of Royal Ascot 2016.

Arm in arm, and a loving glance between the couple at Broadlands, Hampshire, on November 18, 2007 – they had honeymooned there 60 years previously and returned to celebrate their diamond wedding at what had been the home of Prince Philip's uncle, Earl Mountbatten.

Surveying some of Her Majesty's kingdom: the Queen and the Duke travel by steam train along the North Antrim coast from Coleraine to Bellarena on June 28, 2016, during the second day of her visit to Northern Ireland to mark her 90th birthday.

A shared moment: June 22, 2016 saw the Queen and the Duke pay a visit to Alder Hey Children's Hospital as part of their tour of Liverpool.

July 5, 2016: the Queen again looks smart in yellow, although it's a different outfit to the one worn for Royal Ascot the previous month, as the couple attend a garden party at the Palace of Holyroodhouse in Edinburgh.

September 1, 1972, saw the Queen and the Duke of Edinburgh visiting a farm on their Balmoral estate, to celebrate their Silver Wedding anniversary.

Royal milestones

In the course of nearly 70 years of marriage, the Queen and the Duke of Edinburgh celebrated and commemorated many significant milestones, both in their family lives and during the course of their public duty.

Among the most recent of these was the Queen's 90th birthday, when the Duke, who was celebrating his own 95th birthday in the same month, accompanied his wife at a number of events to mark her official birthday in June 2016 – her actual birthday is April 21.

The Duke's 90th birthday was celebrated in 2011, when former Conservative Prime Minister David Cameron

and his wife Samantha hosted a lunch at Downing Street for the royal couple.

Back in 1997, the Queen and Prince Philip were also guests at Number 10 when Labour's Prime Minister of the day, Tony Blair, and his wife Cherie organised a celebratory lunch to mark the golden wedding anniversary of the Queen and her consort.

Having celebrated historic milestones as a couple, they were no doubt delighted to be in good health in order to commemorate together the centenary of the Battle of the Somme at a service at Westminster Abbey on June 30, 2016, the venue for the couple's wedding on November 20, 1947.

September 1, 1972: the Queen and the Duke of Edinburgh at Balmoral, the royal residence in West Aberdeenshire, Scotland, marking their Silver Wedding anniversary.

The Duke of Edinburgh, emerging from the Channel Tunnel at Coquelles, near Calais, on April 3, 1992, was the first member of the royal family to travel from England to France through the Channel Tunnel. With him are Sir Alastair Morton (second right), chief executive of Eurotunnel, and David Bell (third right), the British Consul General from Lille. Prince Philip took three hours 20 minutes to make the 50km journey, which would take just 35 minutes when the tunnel had its first fare-paying customer in 1993.

The Duke of Edinburgh and Cherie Blair, wife of Prime Minister Tony Blair, in good spirits during the Queen and Duke's golden wedding anniversary lunch, hosted by Mr Blair, who paid a heartfelt personal tribute to the Queen, at the Banqueting House, on November 20, 1997.

March 22, 1996: The Queen watches as the Duke of Edinburgh feeds a bird during their visit to the Wildfowl and Wetlands Trust to celebrate the 50th anniversary of the founding of the Wildfowl Trust in Slimbridge.

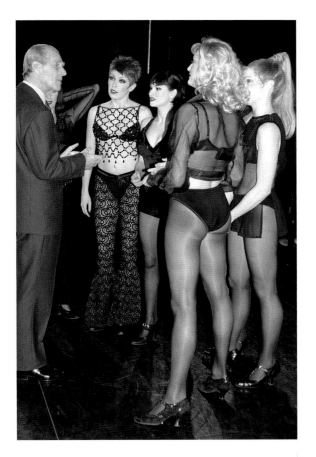

March 4, 1999 – The Duke talks with members of the award-winning West End musical Chicago. The Duke made a 40-minute visit to the Adelphi Theatre to see a full dress rehearsal of the sell-out 1920s jazz musical, part of a tour of London's Theatreland with the Queen.

US President George W Bush walks with the Duke of Edinburgh during an inspection of the Guard of Honour from the 1st Bn Grenadier Guards, for the official American State ceremony taking place at Buckingham Palace on November 19, 2003. Traditional British pomp and ceremony, including a 41-gun salute, was laid on for the start of the historic state visit. The President and Mrs Bush stayed overnight at the Palace before the official welcome ceremony.

Former Prime Minister David Cameron and his wife Samantha pose with Prince Philip and the Queen outside 10 Downing Street in London on Tuesday, June 21, 2011. The Prime Minister and Mrs Cameron hosted a lunch at Downing Street for the Queen and the Duke of Edinburgh to celebrate the Duke's 90th birthday.

The couple appeared on the balcony at Buckingham Palace for the Queen's 90th birthday celebrations in June 2016.

The Prince arrives at the Patron's Lunch as part of the Queen's 90th celebrations.

The Queen and Duke travel along the Mall in an open-topped Range Rover during the Queen's birthday celebrations.

The Duke, pictured with the Queen and Archbishop of Canterbury at a National Service of Thanksgiving on his 95th birthday, June 10, 2016, at St Paul's Cathedral.

Sunshine on The Mall as the Duke and the Queen travel in an open-topped vehicle with younger members of the Royal Family during the Queen's birthday celebrations in June 2016.

The Queen and the Duke during a service to commemorate the centenary of the Battle of the Somme at Westminster Abbey in London on June 30, 2016.

Did you know...?

The steadfast Duke was at the forefront of many organisations after taking on his role in public life. In addition to travelling, with and without the Queen, to dozens of countries during her record-breaking reign, he has fulfilled thousands of official duties and been patron of many charities and organisations.

So, did you know...

* When David Cameron tendered his resignation on July 13, 2016, the Duke had witnessed 12 British Prime Ministers come and go since his marriage to the Queen.

* There have also been 12 US Presidents since the Queen and the Duke became engaged, with the outgoing President, Barack Obama, and his wife Michelle enjoying a memorable meeting with the senior British royals at Buckingham Palace in 2009.

* Until 2011, the Duke was Chancellor of both the University of Cambridge (since 1976) and the University of Edinburgh (since 1952). He also served as Chancellor of the Universities of Salford (1967-91) and Wales (1948-76).

* The Duke learned to fly a range of different aircraft types. He gained his RAF wings in 1953, his helicopter wings in 1956 and his private pilot's licence in 1959, achieving 5986 hours in 59 types. His final flight was on August 11, 1997 from Carlisle to Islay, following which he stopped flying.

* The first official overseas visit with the Queen was the coronation tour of the Commonwealth from November 1953 to May 1954, when they visited countries in the Caribbean, Australasia, Ceylon, Africa and Europe, travelling a distance of 43,618 miles.

* Until 1999, Prince Philip was a member of the House of Lords but never spoke there owing to his proximity to the Queen, who remains politically neutral.

* The Duke was only the fifth consort to a reigning queen in British history. Prince Albert was created Prince Consort by Queen Victoria – who was the great-great-grandmother of both the Queen and the Duke – in 1857.

* In 2001 alone, he undertook 363 solo engagements in the UK and abroad.

* Care of the environment was one of the Duke's greatest interests. He was the first President of the World Wildlife Fund-UK from its foundation in 1961 to 1982, and was International President of WWF from 1981 to 1996. He has visited WWF projects in more than 40 countries on five continents.

* Naval history was always a keen interest too, and he was appointed a trustee of the National Maritime Museum in 1948. He was instrumental in saving the tea clipper *Cutty Sark* – now a museum ship stationed in Greenwich – and in establishing the Maritime Trust. The Duke also had a strong interest in the welfare of ex-servicemen and women.

* He was the first member of the royal family to be interviewed on television, in May 1961.

* The Duke travelled widely without the Queen during his naval and public working lives. He made two round-the-world voyages in the Royal Yacht *Britannia*, visiting some of the remotest parts of the Commonwealth as the Queen's representative, travelling some 72,430 miles by *Britannia*, whose interior he helped to design. The four-month voyage of 1956-57 included visits to the remote South Atlantic locations of the Falkland Islands, South Georgia, Tristan da Cunha, Ascension Island and St Helena.

* Prince Philip lived for seven years in France as a boy, and could speak the language well.

* From 1952 to 1999 the Duke served as President of the Royal Mint Advisory Committee on the design of coins, seals and medals.

* The islanders of Tanna, one of the islands in Vanuatu in the South West Pacific, worship the Duke of Edinburgh as a god.

* The Duke's eight grandchildren are Peter Phillips, Zara Phillips, Prince William, Prince Harry, Princess Beatrice, Princess Eugenie, Lady Louise Windsor and James, Viscount Severn. Five great-grandchildren include the Duke and Duchess of Cambridge's children Prince George and Princess Charlotte.

Naval niftiness: April 1, 1955 saw the Duke transferring ships by jackstay, during the Home Fleet's passage home from Malta after the combined naval exercises in the Mediterranean.

An early trip abroad. Princess Elizabeth, accompanied by the Duke of Edinburgh, looks over Valletta from the roof of the Villa Guardamangia, Malta, on November 25, 1949. The Duke was serving as a First Lieutenant aboard HMS *Chequers*.

The Duke of Edinburgh made a round-the-world tour aboard the Royal Yacht *Britannia*. He is pictured feeding penguins during a visit to the Antarctic on January 7, 1957.

The Queen and the Duke take photographs during their visit to the South Sea Islands of Tuvalu on October 26, 1982.

A historic moment: South African President Nelson Mandela, accompanied by his daughter Princess Zenani Mandela-Dlamini, stands with the Queen and Duke of Edinburgh in the Music Room of Buckingham Palace before a state banquet in the president's honour. The picture was taken on July 9, 1996.

March 1, 2002: this was an occasion referred to in Chapter 11, as the Queen and the Duke watched a culture show at Tjapukai Aboriginal Culture Park, Cairns, Australia. The Duke surprised the aborigines when he asked them "Do you still throw spears at each other?"

Grandfatherly advice: The Duke speaks to Prince William and Prince Harry at Sandhurst Royal Military Academy after The Sovereign's Parade that marked the completion of Prince Harry's Officer training on April 12, 2006.

In robes and wearing a mortarboard the Duke, Cambridge University Chancellor, is pictured in the courtyard at Senate House, Cambridge before a university graduation ceremony on June 27, 2006.

Carla Bruni and the Duke of Edinburgh share a joke as she and her husband Nicolas Sarkozy watch the ceremonial welcome at Windsor Castle with the Queen on March 26, 2008. As a child, Prince Philip spent seven years in France living near Paris with his uncle. On a state visit in 2008, the then French first lady Carla Bruni-Sarkozy marvelled at his "impeccable French".

US President Barack Obama and his wife, Michelle, are welcomed to Buckingham Palace on April 1, 2009.

June 13, 2009

My man in uniform! On Horse Guards Parade during the annual Trooping the Colour parade.

Working well into retirement

There will be few men in this country – or anywhere in the world – who are in their nineties yet will still be happy to get out of bed and spend a day at work. But this is a habit that the Duke of Edinburgh has found hard to break, as he and the Queen have continued fulfilling their royal duties long after most people their age would have hung up their working clothes.

So here we celebrate some of the events that the Queen and the Duke attended after the arrival of the 21st century – many from the summer of 2016 when the Queen celebrated her 90th birthday – which show the variety of events they have attended and, in some cases, the distances they have travelled to deliver some joy into the lives of people, often many decades younger, who turned out to see them.

March 24, 2005

The annual Royal Maundy Service which took place at Wakefield Cathedral, West Yorkshire, in 2005.

July 2, 2007

The couple are pictured during the official reopening of Baxter Park and pavilion in Dundee.

July 6, 2016

The Queen is accompanied by her husband as she officially opens the Slessor Gardens event space in Dundee on the sixth day of a visit to Scotland.

August 19, 2001

October 25, 2005

The Duke with Camilla, the Duchess of Cornwall, arriving to pose for a photograph with Norway's Crown Princess Mette-Marit, Norway's Crown Prince Haakon, Norway's Queen Sonja and King Harald V, with the Queen and Prince Charles before attending a banquet inside Buckingham Palace to mark the centenary of Norwegian independence from Sweden.

The Duke enjoys the speeches at the opening ceremony for the America's Cup Jubilee in Cowes, Isle of Wight. The cup and more than 200 yachts, including many former winners, were on the island for the regatta, which celebrated 150 years of the famous race.

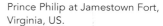

Prince Philip at Jamestown Fort, Virginia, US.

May 4, 2007

November 24, 2005

Prince Philip holds up an umbrella for his wife before she unveiled a plinth to inaugurate the Grand Harbour Marina in Vittoriosa, during her state visit to Malta, where she attended the four-day Commonwealth Heads of Government Meeting on the island in her role as head of the Commonwealth.

July 9, 2014

The Duke in reflective mood during a Service of Dedication to Admiral Arthur Philip at Westminster Abbey.

April 21, 2016

The Queen and the Duke ride an open top Range Rover in Windsor, Berkshire, as she celebrates her 90th birthday.

Sheltering from the rain – the Duke takes cover under an umbrella in the garden of Buckingham Palace, as up to 8000 guests attend the first royal garden party of the year.

May 10, 2016

May 15, 2016

The Duke attends the fifth day of the Royal Windsor Horse Show at Windsor Castle in Berkshire.

The Queen is accompanied by the Duke as she leaves St Paul's Cathedral in London following a national service of thanksgiving to celebrate her 90th birthday.

June 2, 2016

The Duke attends the Rifles' Sounding Retreat on Horse Guards Parade in London, where he took the salute, as the Massed Bands and Bugles of the Rifles return to Horse Guards after nearly 25 years.

June 10, 2016

June 30, 2016

The royal couple lay a wreath on the Grave of the Unknown Warrior during a service to commemorate the centenary of the Battle of the Somme at Westminster Abbey in London.

The Duke of Edinburgh in the parade ring before the opening race on day two of Royal Ascot 2016, at Ascot Racecourse.

June 15, 2016

July 2, 2016

Emerging following the opening of the fifth session of the Scottish Parliament in Edinburgh.

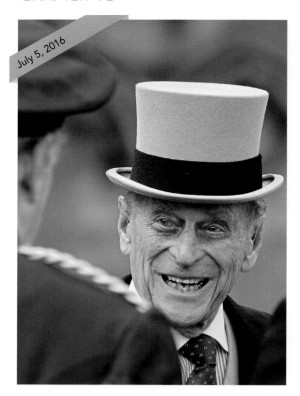

July 5, 2016

July 6, 2016

The Queen unveiled a plaque during a visit to the Leverhulme Research Centre for Forensic Science at Dundee University, and is pictured with the Duke having a closer look afterwards.

July 14, 2016

Together during a reception for the winners of The Queen's Awards for Enterprise 2016 at Buckingham Palace.

The Duke attends a garden party at the Palace of Holyroodhouse in Edinburgh.

The couple arrive at St Giles' Cathedral in Edinburgh for the Order of the Thistle Service.

July 7, 2016

July 8, 2016

The Duke of Edinburgh views master chaser and silversmith Panos Kirkos at work during a visit to Hamilton and Inches jewellers in Edinburgh with the Queen, where they viewed a display of artefacts and met craftsmen, including some who were part of the Queen Elizabeth Scholarship Trust founded to allow promising young people to develop their skills by working with masters of their craft.

July 8, 2016

The couple view the Queens Cup which is presented at the Calcutta Races in India, during a visit to Hamilton and Inches jewellers in Edinburgh.

The Duke on board a Land Rover BAR catamaran during his visit to the America's Cup challenger in Portsmouth.

July 22, 2016

The Prince of Wales and his bride Camilla, Duchess of Cornwall, with the Duke of Edinburgh and other members of the Royal Family as they leave St George's Chapel in Windsor following the church blessing of Charles and Camilla's civil wedding ceremony on April 9, 2005.

The future of the monarchy

New generations are ready to take over the royal mantle from the Queen and the Duke of Edinburgh, as this series of delightful pictures shows. The close and loving relationship between Prince William, the Duke of Cambridge, and his paternal grandparents is clear to see.

Whether on 'home turf' – the picturesque settings of St George's Chapel in the grounds of Windsor Castle, or the balcony of Buckingham Palace, for example – or further afield on public engagements, the Queen and the Duke of Edinburgh have demonstrated their commitment to their family and their country with kindness, warm smiles and good humour.

And like any proud grandparents and great-grandparents, they have enjoyed attending events that the younger generations have been involved in, especially those that focus on weddings and

christenings – celebrations that pull the strands of the family tighter together.

With a large family around them, the Queen and the Duke are the hub and the beating heart of the House of Windsor; bright twin suns in a royal universe spreading outwards across new generations and fresh styles of leadership. They saw not only their own four children have children, but some of those children also have families of their own – most notably Prince William, father of Prince George and Princess Charlotte, following his marriage to Catherine, Duchess of Cambridge.

In this final chapter we capture some of the magical moments from the family album and images that illustrate the enduring appeal of Elizabeth II and Philip… a royal romance that became an international success story.

The Queen, the Duke of Edinburgh and the Prince of Wales leave the Chapel Royal in St James's Palace, central London on October 23, 2013, following the christening of Prince George by the Archbishop of Canterbury.

Three generations: Prince Philip, Duke of Edinburgh, with his grandson Prince Harry and only daughter Princess Anne on the balcony of Buckingham Palace on June 17, 2006.

The Duke of Edinburgh watches with pleasure as the Queen receives flowers from children as she leaves the Easter Day service at St George's Chapel in the grounds of Windsor Castle on March 23, 2013.

Princess Beatrice, elder daughter of Prince Andrew, the Duke of York, outside St George's Chapel in Windsor after the marriage of her cousin Peter Phillips to Autumn Kelly.

St George's Chapel in Windsor was the venue for the wedding of the Queen and the Duke's eldest grandchild, Peter Phillips, and Autumn Kelly on May 17, 2008.

Family celebration: enjoyment for (left to right) the Duchess of Cambridge, the Duke of Edinburgh, Peter Phillips, the Queen and the Duke of Cambridge in the Royal Box for the Patron's Lunch in The Mall, central London, in honour of the Queen's 90th birthday.

The Duchess of Cambridge and Duke of Edinburgh watch the Patron's Parade along The Mall, during the Patron's Lunch in central London in honour of the Queen's 90th birthday – June 12, 2016.

Prince William, the Duke of Cambridge, walks with his grandparents across the East Anglian Air Ambulance base at Cambridge Airport.

A kiss for grandmother: the Queen is dwarfed by her grandson, the Duke of Cambridge, as the Duke of Edinburgh looks on. The couple opened the new base of East Anglian Air Ambulance at Cambridge Airport on July 13, 2016.

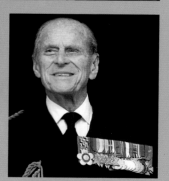

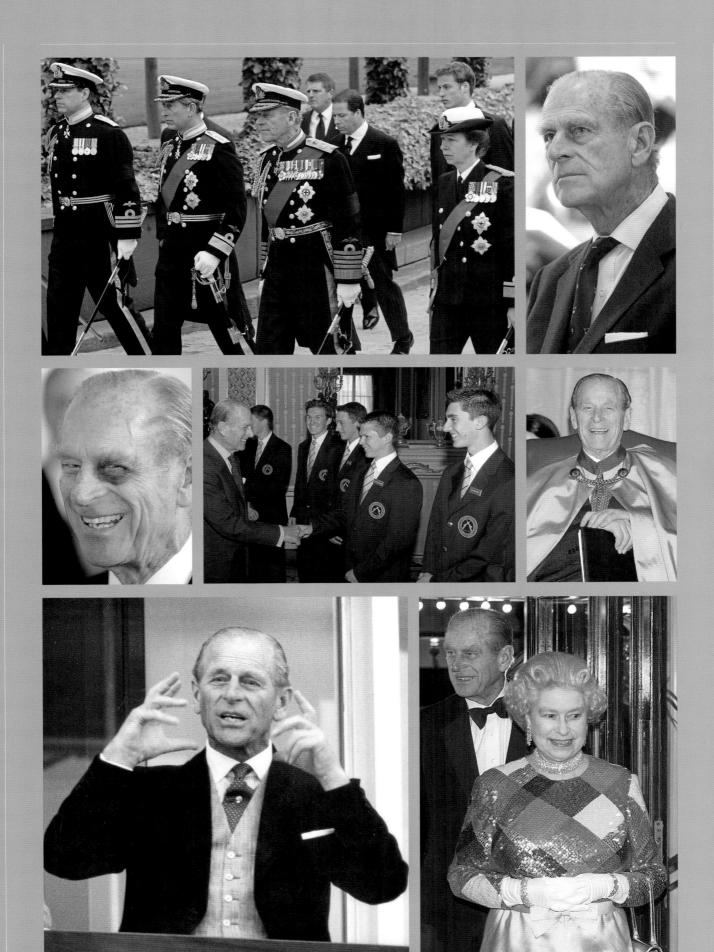

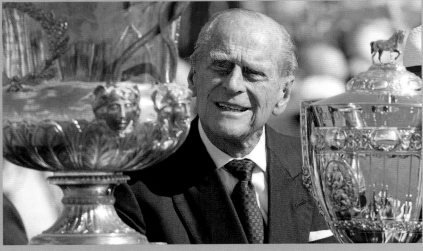

The Duke of Edinburgh on a visit to Halifax, Nova Scotia, in June 2010, where he presented a medal from the World Ship Trust to Alan Latourelle, who received it on behalf of Parks Canada.